D1524369

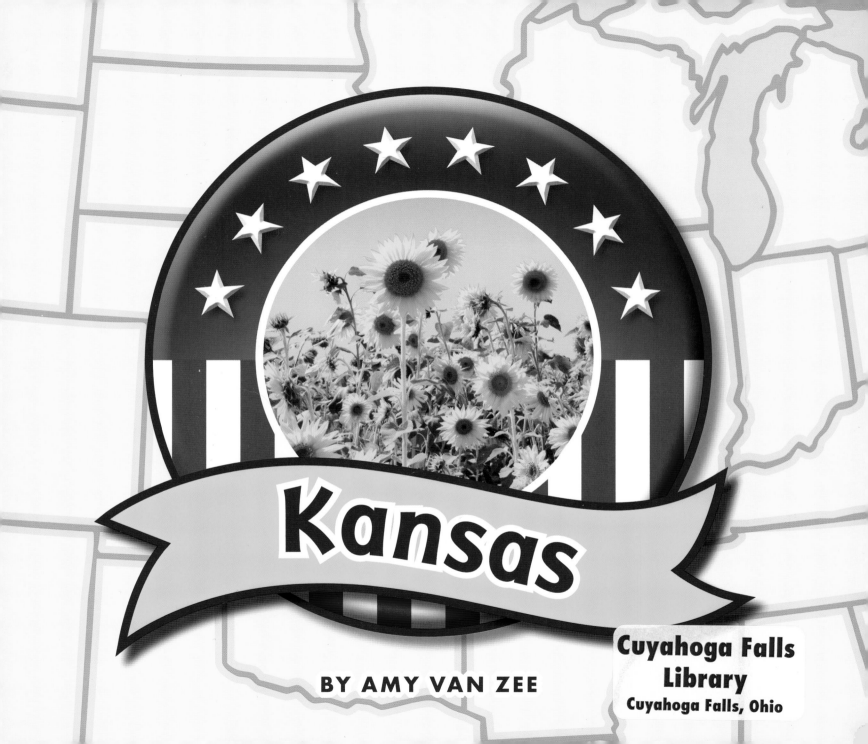

Kansas

BY AMY VAN ZEE

Published by The Child's World®
1980 Lookout Drive • Mankato, MN 56003-1705
800-599-READ • www.childsworld.com

ACKNOWLEDGMENTS
The Child's World®: Mary Berendes, Publishing Director
The Design Lab: Design and production
Red Line Editorial: Editorial direction

PHOTO CREDITS: Lukiyanova Natalia/Shutterstock Images, cover, 1, 3;
Matt Kania/Map Hero, Inc., 4, 5; Lawrence Sawyer/iStockphoto, 7; Ricardo
Reitmeyer/iStockphoto, 9; iStockphoto, 10; Tracy Tucker/iStockphoto, 11;
Levent Songur/iStockphoto, 13; Library of Congress, 15; Travis Morisse/AP
Images, 17; AP Images, 19; Chad Jackson/iStockphoto, 21; One Mile Up,
22; Quarter-dollar coin image from the United States Mint, 22

LIBRARY OF CONGRESS CATALOGING-IN-PUBLICATION DATA
Van Zee, Amy.
  Kansas / by Amy Van Zee.
    p. cm.
  Includes bibliographical references and index.
  ISBN 978-1-60253-460-5 (library bound : alk. paper)
  1. Kansas—Juvenile literature. I. Title.

F681.3.V36 2010
978.1—dc22

                    2010017711

Printed in the United States of America in Mankato, Minnesota.
July 2010
F11538

On the cover:
Kansas is called
"the Sunflower
State."

CONTENTS

4 Geography

6 Cities

8 Land

10 Plants and Animals

12 People and Work

14 History

16 Ways of Life

18 Famous People

20 Famous Places

22 *State Symbols*

23 *Glossary*

24 *Further Information*

24 *Index*

Geography

Let's explore Kansas! Kansas is in the central United States. This area is called the Midwest. The Missouri River makes the northeastern border of Kansas.

The geographical center of the mainland of the United States is located in Kansas. It is near Smith Center.

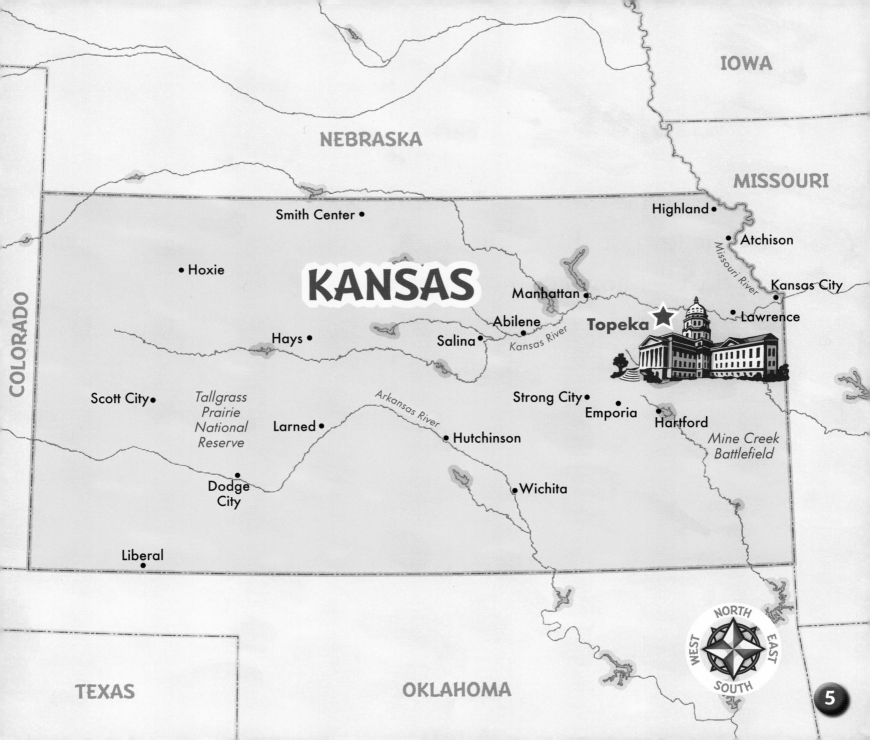

IOWA

NEBRASKA

MISSOURI

Smith Center •

Highland •

• Atchison

Hoxie •

KANSAS

Manhattan •

Kansas City

Abilene •

Topeka ★

• Lawrence

Hays •

Salina •

Kansas River

COLORADO

Scott City •

Tallgrass Prairie National Reserve

Strong City •

• Emporia

Arkansas River

Larned •

• Hartford

Dodge City •

• Hutchinson

Mine Creek Battlefield

• Wichita

Liberal •

NORTH

WEST   EAST

TEXAS

OKLAHOMA

SOUTH

Cities

Topeka is the capital of Kansas. Wichita is the largest city in the state. Kansas City is a well-known city in Kansas.

About 120,000 people live in Topeka. ▶

Land

The eastern part of Kansas is mostly **prairies**. The western part of the state is high **plains**. Some parts of Kansas have tall hills and deep valleys. The Arkansas River and the Kansas River run through the state.

Kansas has many grass prairies. ▶

Plants and Animals

The state tree of Kansas is the cottonwood. This type of poplar tree is good for shade. Kansas's state flower is the sunflower. It has yellow **petals** and a brown center. The state bird is the western meadowlark. These birds are usually brown and black.

Sunflowers grow about three to 15 feet (.9–4.6 m) tall. ▶

People and Work

More than 2.8 million people live in Kansas. Many people work in farming. Farmers here grow wheat, corn, and sunflowers. Hogs and cattle are raised here, too. Other people work in **manufacturing**. Many make computer parts.

Many airplanes are built in Kansas.

Some workers in Kansas make **equipment**. ▶

History

Explorers from Spain came to the area that is now Kansas in the 1500s. At the time, many Native Americans lived on the land. Kansas became a U.S. **territory** in 1854. It became the thirty-fourth state on January 29, 1861.

Native Americans from the Comanche **tribe** have called the Kansas area home. ▶

In the 1800s, more than 10,000 Native Americans from dozens of tribes moved to the land that is now Kansas. They were forced to leave their homes in other areas of the United States. When white settlers later came to the Kansas area, they took back much of the land from the Native Americans.

Ways of Life

Many people fish and boat on Kansas lakes. Hunting is another **popular** activity. Many people in Kansas also enjoy music, art, and going to **theaters**.

The lakes in Kansas are good places for fishing. ▶

Famous People

Amelia Earhart was born in Kansas. She was the first woman to fly an airplane across the Atlantic Ocean. Walter Percy Chrysler was also born here. He started the Chrysler **Corporation** that makes cars. Former football player Barry Sanders was born in Kansas, too.

Amelia Earhart was born in Atchison, Kansas. ▶

Famous Places

Kansas has many national parks. Workers in the parks care for prairies and **grasslands**. People can camp and see animals here. The Mine Creek Battlefield was the site of a large U.S. **Civil War** battle. The Pawnee Indian **Museum** tells the story of the Native American group that has lived in the Kansas area for many years.

The Tallgrass Prairie National Reserve is a large area in Kansas. The Flint Hills is one of the last ▶ remaining tallgrass prairies in North America.

State Symbols

Seal

The Kansas state seal shows a rising sun. A man plowing the land with horses stands for the state's farming. Go to childsworld.com/links for a link to Kansas's state Web site, where you can get a firsthand look at the state seal.

Flag

The state flag has the state seal. In the seal, people are traveling in covered wagons.

Quarter

An American buffalo is on the Kansas state quarter. The American buffalo is the state animal. Sunflowers are also on the quarter. It came out in 2005.

Glossary

Civil War (SIV-il WOR): In the United States, the Civil War was a war fought between the Northern and the Southern states from 1861 to 1865. A large Civil War battle took place in Kansas.

corporation (kor-puh-RAY-shun): A corporation is a company run by a group of people. Walter P. Chrysler, who founded the Chrysler Corporation, was born in Kansas.

equipment (ih-KWIP-munt): Equipment is the set of items needed to do something. Transportation equipment is produced in Kansas.

grasslands (GRASS-landz): Grasslands are large, open areas of grass. Some workers in Kansas take care of grasslands.

mainland (MAYN-lund): A mainland is the main part of a landmass that is usually separated by water from islands or peninsulas. The geographical center of the mainland of the United States is in Kansas.

manufacturing (man-yuh-FAK-chur-ing): Manufacturing is the task of making items with machines. Manufacturing is done in Kansas.

museum (myoo-ZEE-um): A museum is a place where people go to see art, history, or science displays. The Pawnee Indian Museum is in Kansas.

petals (PET-ulz): Petals are the colorful parts of flowers. The petals of a sunflower, the Kansas state flower, are yellow.

plains (PLAYNZ): Plains are areas of flat land that do not have many trees. The western part of Kansas is made of plains.

popular (POP-yuh-lur): To be popular is to be enjoyed by many people. Hunting is popular in Kansas.

prairies (PRAYR-eez): Prairies are flat or hilly grasslands. The eastern part of Kansas is made of prairies.

seal (SEEL): A seal is a symbol a state uses for government business. The Kansas seal has a man plowing on it.

symbols (SIM-bulz): Symbols are pictures or things that stand for something else. The seal and flag are symbols of Kansas.

territory (TAYR-uh-tor-ee): A territory is a piece of land that is controlled by another country. Kansas became a U.S. territory in 1854.

theaters (thee-IT-urz): Theaters are buildings where movies and plays are shown. People enjoy going to the theaters in Kansas.

tribe (TRYB): A tribe is a group of people who share ancestors and customs. The Comanche is a Native American tribe that has lived in Kansas.

Further Information

Books

Blanton, Lynne, and Betsy Hedberg. *States*. Lincolnwood, IL: Publications International, 2002.

Scillian, Devin, and Corey Scillian. *S is for Sunflower: A Kansas Alphabet*. Chelsea, MI: Sleeping Bear Press, 2004.

Taylor-Butler, Christine. *Kansas*. New York: Children's Press, 2006.

Web Sites

Visit our Web site for links about Kansas: *childsworld.com/links*

Note to Parents, Teachers, and Librarians: We routinely verify our Web links to make sure they are safe and active sites. So encourage your readers to check them out!

Index

activities, 16
Arkansas River, 8
capital, 6
Earhart, Amelia, 18
jobs, 12
Kansas River, 8

Midwest, 4
Mine Creek Battlefield, 20
Missouri River, 4
Native Americans, 14, 20
Pawnee Indian Museum, 20

population, 12
state bird, 10
state flower, 10
state tree, 10
tourism, 20
U.S. Civil War, 20